A Book About My Sister

A Sibling's Creation

Randi L. Millward

Instructions:

This book is a children's activity book. The sentences are started but left incomplete for the child to finish in his or her own words. The adjacent pages are intentionally left blank for the child to illustrate with his or her own personal artwork.

The artist may color with crayons, tape photos onto the paper, or use any other age-appropriate parent-approved artistic medium that does not bleed through the paper.

Disclaimer: Author/Publisher not responsible for any loss or damage to anyone or anything caused by or related to the use of this book or any medium used in or on this book. Parents bear the sole responsibility for their child(ren)'s safety.

ISBN-10: 0989486540
ISBN-13: 978-0-9894865-4-5

More books by this author may be found online at
www.Amazon.com

A Book About My Sister

By

____

Age: ______________

Date: ______________

My sister is

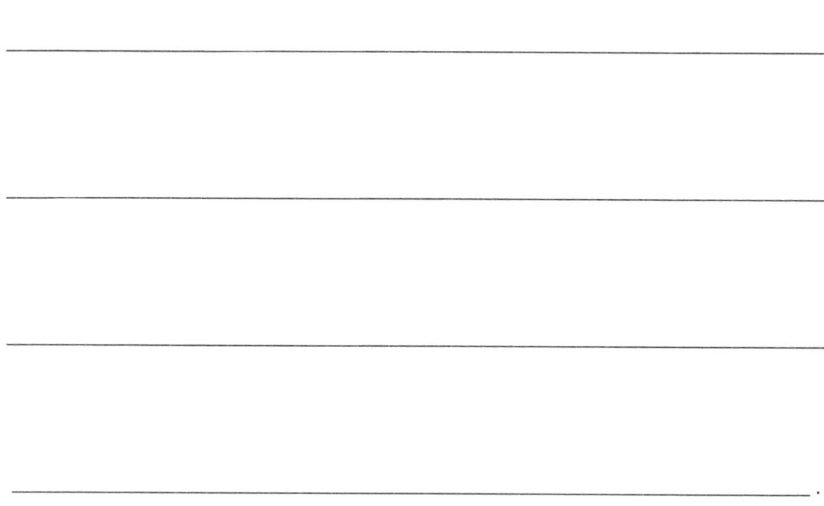

My sister has

____

____

____

____________________________________.

I like when my sister

____

____

____

______________________________.

My sister likes when I

____

____

____

______________________________________.

My sister doesn't like

____

____

____

______________________________.

My sister is really good at

____

____

____

_______________________________________.

My sister says

My sister smiles when I

I have fun when my sister and I

____

____

____

____________________________________.

My sister laughs when

____

____

____

______________________________________.

My favorite thing to do with my sister is

____

____

____

___________________________________.

My favorite thing to play with my sister is

____

____

____

______________________________.

I hope that someday my sister

____

____

____

______________________________________.

I get excited when my sister

____

____

____

________________________________.

When I am sad, my sister

____

____

____

____.

My favorite thing about my sister is

____

____

____

______________________________.

I love my sister because

The End

www.ingramcontent.com/pod-product-compliance
Lightning Source LLC
LaVergne TN
LVHW010946110826
845149LV00013B/2773
* 9 7 8 0 9 8 9 4 8 6 5 4 5 *